Interview Questions

~

Great Tips on How to Get Ready for a Job Interview. 30 Great Answers to Common Behavioral Interview Questions.

Samuel Morgan

Copyright © 2015 Jane Morgan

All rights reserved.

ISBN: 1514624931
ISBN-13: 978-1514624937

TABLE OF CONTENTS

	Introduction	4
1	The Importance of Being Earnest	7
2	Navigating the Hiring Process	10
3	Let's Get Physical	15
4	Going Emotional	19
5	Mental Strength	22
6	Interview Basics	25
7	Answering Behavioral Interview Questions	29
	Conclusion	39

Introduction

I want to thank you and congratulate you for purchasing the book, *"Interview Questions: **Great Tips on How to Get Ready for a Job Interview. 30 Great Answers to Common Behavioral Interview Questions**"*

This book contains steps and ideas on how to make a career breakthrough by acing any job interview. Whether you are a fresh graduate seeking your first job, an experienced professional planning for a career shift, a productive worker aiming to get a big promotion, or a manager who wants to take a big leap and get that dream job in a reputable company, you would have to go through a rigorous application process that would inevitably include an interview.

By reading this book, you'll get some valuable insights into how you can best prepare for the interview. Each chapter is full of great tips that you could use to ensure a successful and interesting discussion with your interviewer. Regardless of whether you'll be facing a single individual or a panel, be prepared with the right frame of mind and great ideas about how you could answer any question thrown at you.

This book discusses the 30 most common behavioral questions that have left many an interview stumped. Avoid the pitfalls of panic, mental block, and stumbling through your words with answers that are sure to make even the toughest interviewer look up and take notice.

Thanks again for purchasing this book. I hope you found it helpful.

Interview Questions

Copyright 2015 by Samuel Morgan. All rights reserved.

This document is geared towards providing exact and reliable information in regards to the topic and issue covered. The publication is sold with the idea that the publisher is not required to render accounting, officially permitted, or otherwise, qualified services. If advice is necessary, legal or professional, a practiced individual in the profession should be ordered.

From a Declaration of Principles which was accepted and approved equally by a Committee of the American Bar Association and a Committee of Publishers and Associations.

In no way is it legal to reproduce, duplicate, or transmit any part of this document in either electronic means or in printed format. Recording of this publication is strictly prohibited and any storage of this document is not allowed unless with written permission from the publisher. All rights reserved.

The information provided herein is stated to be truthful and consistent, in that any liability, in terms of inattention or otherwise, by any usage or abuse of any policies, processes, or directions contained within is the solitary and utter responsibility of the recipient reader. Under no circumstances will any legal responsibility or blame be held against the publisher for any reparation, damages, or monetary loss due to the information herein, either directly or indirectly.

Respective authors own all copyrights not held by the publisher.

The information herein is offered for informational purposes solely, and is universal as so. The presentation of the information is without contract or any type of guarantee assurance.

The trademarks that are used are without any consent, and the publication of the trademark is without permission or backing by the trademark owner. All trademarks and brands within this book are for clarifying purposes only and are the owned by the owners themselves, not affiliated with this document.

CHAPTER 1

The Importance of Being Earnest

It's a Wild World Out There

With the sheer number of people graduating each year, there is no question why the job market is increasingly becoming crowded. Students who are graduating significantly outnumber the people who are resigning or retiring. As a direct result, a large surplus of workers exists, as opposed to a significant shortage of available jobs.

This shortage of job supply has made the job market highly competitive. There are so many people vying for position, from the entry level up to the highest echelons of management. It is thus no wonder why many jobseekers have to feel the pain of rejection and consequently lose the drive and motivation to look for the next opportunity and do well throughout the application process.

The best step to take is to go about the process with determination. Give yourself zero room for failure, and always reach beyond your potential. After all, the greatest rewards are obtained after all the word work is done.

Job Hunting in Earnest

Now that you know how stiff the competition is, you might have already realized that deciding to go job hunting can somewhat be likened to a leap of faith. For fresh graduates who only have knowledge gained from school and maybe some part-time work experience in their arsenal, the prospect of looking for a job may be daunting. Similarly, even seasoned professionals who are aiming for a career shift or a jump up the career ladder may feel intimidated by going through the entire hiring process again.

So what's the bottom line? Everyone is in the same boat when trying to look for a job. Fresh graduates may have limited to nil interview experience, but long-term workers may not have gone to an interview for years. This makes the tips outlined in the succeeding chapters highly valuable for anyone who is joining or currently struggling in the corporate world.

An important thing to remember is that job hunting should be done in earnest. Seeking employment is a serious business, and it will serve you best to keep in mind that hiring managers, line managers, and the other people whom you would be dealing with during the hiring process are looking for someone who has not only the skill set needed for the position, but also the attitude and outlook necessary to ensure job success. This makes job hunting a serious business that should never be taken lightly.

Useful Statistics

A common mistake made by many job hunters is setting unreasonable deadlines for them to land their dream job. As a job seeker, you have to remember a couple of useful statistics so that you can properly set your frame of mind while on your quest to land your dream job.

- Out of the millions of jobs made available each year, approximately 80% have gone unadvertised. What this means for job seekers is that it is best to build a great professional network or even make your resume available online so that you can be made aware of suitable positions through word of mouth, or you can be headhunted by recruitment managers.

- On average, more than 100 people apply to any open position. Of all these applicants, less than 25% are able to secure an interview. What this means for you is that your resume should be optimized by highlighting how your qualifications and credentials best fit the job description. Gone are the days when you can send out a generic curriculum vitae to any open position that is advertised. It would serve you well to tailor fit your resume for every job opening that you are interested in. A resume is important so that you can get your foot in the door. However, do not be complacent; 25% means approximately 25 people get to be interviewed, so you still remain as one of the many fish in the pool. The next chapters will help you ensure that you the biggest one in that pool.

- In general, interviews last for approximately 40 minutes. An average individual would have been able to compose himself or herself within the first 10 minutes. Make sure that you subdue your panic and rise to the occasion as a competent professional.

- The hiring process is increasingly becoming longer and is starting to include more steps. A test, an interview, another interview, an on-the-job task, a company tour, a couple more interviews—it can seem endless if you are not patient. After an interview is concluded, it can take anywhere from one day, two weeks, to one month before you hear from a prospective employer again. Be patient, and use that waiting time wisely to brush up for the next steps.

With these statistics in mind, you are well on your way to being ready for the hiring process. The next chapter will detail how you can navigate the increasingly complex maze that is the hiring process.

CHAPTER 2

Navigating the Hiring Process

To the uninitiated, the application and hiring process would most likely be confusing and intimidating. Well, the good news is that this need not be the case. In this chapter, you will find a step-by-step guide to help you understand all the steps that you would have to undergo to be able to land that dream job.

Identify your niche and find suitable vacancies

You can consider the application and hiring process as something similar to match making in that your skill set has to match the requirements of a prospective employer for a certain position. This is why as an important first step, you should be able to identify your niche—your skills and what you are good at.

You cannot simply find a vacancy and then immediate shoot an email to the hiring manager. You should not be trigger happy with that send button! Identifying the skills that you have and then finding a vacancy that would need the same skills would increase your chances of success without having to spend a great deal of time, effort, and resources.

Passing the Paper Screening

Paper screening is the tradition term used for when a prospective employer takes a look at your resume and verified whether there is a potential match with the requirements. This is why you should take great care in preparing a professional, well-written cover letter and a resume that highlights your strengths and clearly shows how your experience can help you contribute to the job.

Remember that over a hundred applicants typically send their resumes for consideration for a single open position. So make sure that your resume is strong enough to help you jockey for position and get your foot in the door going toward the next step.

Acing the Examination

Not all vacancies require that applicants take a pen-and-paper or practical examination. Nevertheless, it is best to be prepared, especially when you are looking to be hired for a technical position. If you are planning to go job hunting, brush up on all your technical skills. Read up on the basics so that if you are asked to take any type of examination, you can surely pass or even excel. Acing an examination is a sure-fire way to get that elusive interview.

Make or Break

Indeed, the interview process is your time in the spotlight. For the majority of vacancies, the interview determines whether you make it through to the next steps or you get rejected for the post.

It is true that your resume can only do so much for your employer to get to know you, your experience, and your background. The resume is "emotionless" in that it does not give your employer a clear picture of who you really are, what your behavior is, what your work philosophy is like, and how well you can potentially go along with people.

The interview provides the prospective employer with an "inside look" into your behavior. Chances are, people who do well in the interview and who could carry on an interesting conversation will likely be able to successfully build good professional relationships within the work place. While it is understandable for many people to be nervous in this situation, being able to compose yourself properly and handle difficult questions lets employers know how well you can handle stress and difficult situations, as well as whether you can make tough decisions, if ever you get the job.

Company Tour or On-the-job Immersion

Although not included in the hiring process of most companies, you may be invited for a site visit, company tour, or on-the-job immersion, all of which are geared toward giving you a feel of the actual work environment. This is particularly true for jobs in production and manufacturing.

This is a great opportunity for you to see whether you will feel comfortable in the work environment offered by the company. This is also a great time to ask questions about the implemented processes and gain insight into how things are actually done. An immersion is also bound to give you ideas as to what needs to be improved and in what areas you could contribute.

The Waiting Game

Perhaps next to the interview, the waiting game is the most excruciating part of any hiring process. Each day without the anticipated call or email is agony. The world seems to stop and life cannot go on. Well, if you start feeling this way, it is time to get a hold on yourself. The key here is patience. Understand that the company only wants to hire the best person for the job. Keep your fingers crossed that the best person is actually you, and resist the urge to spam the hiring manager for any updates about the status of your application.

The Golden Ticket

This, of course, refers to the offer of employment. Many applicants dream of the moment during which they sign their name on the dotted line with a flourish. If you come to this point, make it a point to pull yourself down from cloud nine to be able to completely understand what is required of you and what you are committing to. A contract is never to be taken lightly, and remember that once you sign that line, you are compelled to do your best in your new position.

Background Checks and Medical Examinations

Most companies have these steps as basic parts of their hiring protocol. Unless you have been convicted or any crime or have any serious medical condition that would hinder you from doing your job properly, then consider yourself good to go.

Now that you have a great idea of what you are likely to go through in your quest toward landing your ideal job, it is time to focus on the most crucial element of the application process—the job interview.

Perhaps none of the other steps require as much preparation, confidence, and mettle as the interview. Having to face someone whom you know nothing about, being placed on the hot seat, and then being grilled about your work experience could be petrifying. But remember that in the same way, the interview also knows nothing about you beyond what you have placed on your resume.

Contrary to popular belief, an interviewee need not be in a position that is subordinate to the interviewer. Although a high level of respect is needed, you could consider an interview to be a meeting of minds—a meeting of equals. Remember that the company needs you as much as you need them. If you match what the company needs, then you have a great chance of landing the job.

The secret here is to be able to present yourself in the best light possible. How do you do that? The answer lies in massive preparation—physical, mental, and emotional. The next chapters will give you great tips on how to literally put your best face forward to increase your chances of interview success.

CHAPTER 3

Let's Get Physical

Physical preparation is very important for a job interview. A lot of people may take this for granted and simply put on a suit and go, expecting that their knowledge and charm will get them where they want to be. However, this underrated aspect of interview preparation needs its time on the spotlight.

Your physical state is known to be a significant determinant of your alertness, focus, and confidence level. Being in a good state of physical well-being is sure to help you better manage the stress that comes along with preparing for a job interview. After all, a sound mind starts from having a sound body.

Below are a few great tips that you should consider in your physical preparation for a job interview.

Rest is priceless

You must have heard this so many times from your parent: Go to sleep! While the urge to party may be strong, trade in your late nights for at least eight hours of sleep. What I am referring to is not just to the day before the interview, but also the days, or even weeks, leading up to the big day.

An ample amount of rest gives you healthier looking skin, gets rids of the dark circles around your eyes, and results in an overall healthy look. Aside from these obvious benefits, a sufficient amount of rest is scientifically proven to enhance your alertness and increase your focus. This means that you can process information faster. You can focus on what the interviewer says, and you can quickly organize your thoughts to come up with a cohesive answer.

Being well-rested enables you to think on your feet, even for answers to the most difficult interview questions. It helps prevent mental block so that you could deliver your answers promptly and clearly. This will definitely give the interviewer the impression that you are well-prepared, focused, and confident, all of which are guaranteed to give you plus points on the interview scorecard.

Good Posture Reflects Confidence

On the days leading up to the interview, you might want to try some simple exercises to improve your posture, such as doing some squats and stretches. A lot of people have the tendency to slouch, and this type of body language can be perceived as negative during an interview.

Slouching and poor posture may give the impression of being evasive, lacking confidence, or even being untruthful. There are warning signs that you would never want to trigger during an interview. Make sure that you have a good posture that radiates confidence and self-assurance. This also extends to your confident strides as you enter the interview room, as well as the firm handshake that you would give.

Brownie Points for Eye Contact

This is a basic for a job interview or even simple conversations that we have with people. Maintaining contact reflects honesty. People who are being truthful are said to be capable of maintaining constant eye contact. However, some individuals, especially those who are very shy, have difficulty maintaining eye contact.

Failure to maintain eye contact may be misconstrued as being untruthful so make sure that you practice this beforehand. It is recommended that you try talking to yourself in the mirror while maintaining eye contact. You can also practice this with friends and family, eventually with acquaintances, to wean you out of your shyness and to make you more confident to look people in the eye while having a conversation.

Practice Good Grooming and Hygiene

A lot of people may roll their eyes on this one, but this is another overlooked interview preparation step. On the day of the interview, be sure to set your alarm up to two hours before you have to leave for your appointment. This will ensure that you will have sufficient time for a shower, shaving for men, brushing your teeth, dressing, and applying make up for women.

Failing to wake up early will surely result in a shortcoming in the grooming department. Rushing through your preparation may cause you to miss some simple grooming steps. Make sure that you look clean and impeccable. Remember that cleanliness is a major factor that contributes to your respectability.

Dress Sharply

This is a given. Be sure to have your best suit or dress dry cleaned and pressed before your interview. Check for any stains, runs, holes, or missing buttons. Remember to dress for success! Being dressed in your best clothes is bound to give you that added boost of confidence to make you feel as if you could conquer the world—or even just the interview for starters.

Minimize the Mannerisms

Are you used to wringing your hands, scratching your nose, or pulling your ear? This is the time to try to control these urges. Mannerisms such as these will make you look nervous or intimidated. What's worse, letting yourself get used to doing these things is bound to place you under greater strain. Try to place your hands on top of each other on your lap, or try to gesture while you're speaking to drive a point home. Trying these simple steps to overcome your mannerisms will definitely make you look more professional.

Meditate

No, you do not need to do those complicated poses. On the minutes leading up to your interview when you feel the most nervous, go to the restroom or any quiet corner. Close your eyes and take deep, even breaths. Control your erratic beating and try to relax to bring your heart rate back to normal. Wipe the sweat off your palms, and try to walk around a little bit to shrug off that nervous energy.

Remember that you would be facing another professional, not a judge or a tyrant. Give your best smile, adopt a positive disposition, listen when needed, organize your thoughts, and answer as honestly as you can. Say it with me: *I am destined for success!*

CHAPTER 4

Going Emotional

Let's face it, emotions almost always get in the way. Be it at home or at work, failing to manage your emotions may lead to more harm than good. The can be said for the interview process.

Passing the paper screening and landing a job interview is to turn up the pressure. For an individual who is weak-willed and easily demotivated, a large amount of pressure may lead to high stress levels or, at worst, a breakdown. Learning how to best manage your emotions and feelings will help you feel more prepared about any upcoming interview.

Away with the negatives

Humans have a natural tendency to always expect the worst. With the prospect of an interview, you may feel queasy and you might start imagining yourself stumbling on your way to the interview room or being stumped at a difficult question. When you find yourself going into this dangerous territory, stop!

Negative thinking incites fear. Keep in mind that there is nothing to fear about in an interview. **Fear** is all in the mind! An interview will just be a pair or a group of normal human beings exchanging ideas in a professional and controlled environment. Fear causes you to choke up and lose focus, and you never want that during an interview.

Another emotion to control is **anxiety**. Remember, an interview is not a life-or-death situation. Do not fall into the trap of all-or-nothing thinking, with you believing that the world would end when you do not get the job. Even failing to ace the interview this time will give you great insight into what you can improve so that you will do better on your succeeding interviews.

While we are on the topic of negatives, let's talk about **intimidation**. I have previously mentioned that you must not think of yourself to be subordinate to an interviewer. Treat the interview as a meeting of equals! Just because you are the one looking for a job does not make you less of a person as compared to the one in front of you. So keep your head up! Remember that you have something great to offer and that the company would benefit from hiring you.

During the interview, you might find yourself grasping for words or stumped by a question because of your nerves. When this happens, do not give in to **frustration** or to **humiliation**. Do not mentally berate yourself for failing to provide a great answer. It happens to the best of us. Also, do not fall into the trap of feeling ashamed of yourself for not meeting your own expectations. If you are stumped by one question, be honest and highlight your strengths. Keep in mind that as long as you are still sitting in that chair, you can still recover and impress your interviewer. One blunder will not cost you the job. It is frustration over one blunder that may break your confidence and your chances.

Positivity for the Win

So now that you know which emotions to control, let's talk about the ones that you need to enhance. First things first, you've got to have **confidence**. Make sure that you have something to bring to the table, and you know it! Having confidence in yourself may lead the interviewer to reflect the same thing and start to believe in that confidence. So nurture that little spark and make it grow.

Another important state of emotion is being **enthusiastic**. Show your interest in the job, and be excited about the prospect of taking on responsibility and being part of the company. Having enthusiasm will infuse your conversation with positivity that is infectious. It can make the conversation an animated one and would definitely help you build rapport with the interviewer.

Finally, be **inspired**! Identify what drives you and what your motivations are, and keep them in mind during the interview. Being inspired will help you set a vision for yourself and your potential. Belief in that potential can make the interviewer take notice and will help you stand out from the crowd. In a sea of gray faces and uninspired people, being the visionary may be enough for you to ace the interview and land the job.

CHAPTER 5

Mental Strength

Probably the most important aspect of preparation that you should engage in is mental conditioning. There is no question that an interview will demand that all your faculties of intellect are engaged and ready. Thinking on your feet, organizing your thought, and forming cohesive answers are processes that you need to master to be able to excel in any interview.

Know Thyself

Of course, this one is already a given. Going into an interview, you should have a keen awareness of who you are, what you love doing, and what you do best. You should know what career path you want to pursue and what goals you want to achieve in the future. A high level of self-awareness will better enable you to present yourself in the best possible light.

Moreover, knowing what your values and principles are will make it easier for you to answer behavioral and situational questions that are bound to arise. Even if a question that can be categorized as tricky comes up, you will never lose your bearings and will be able to provide an honest answer that is bound to impress your interviewer.

Research, Research, Research

When preparing for an interview, it is not enough that you know what your strengths and accomplishments are. It is also very important to conduct research about the company. Knowing the company's culture, vision, and work environment will enable you to better explain why you applied for the position and why you would like to stay with the company for the long term.

Researching about the company will also reaffirm how serious you are about pursuing the position. It shows that you have a high level of interest in learning about what the company does and how you can best contribute to its success.

Raise Your Own Questions

In relation to the above suggestion on conducting research about the company, you would probably have some questions pop into your head about a variety of aspects, from something as complex as agile methodologies to something as simple as leave credits. Make sure that you take note of all these questions because you just might have the opportunity to ask them during the interview.

One very important thing to remember is that in an interview, you're not just there to answer questions. It is a highly interactive discussion, which means that there is room for you to ask questions, too. Asking questions during an interview will let the interviewer know that you are actively engaged in the discussion and are committed to being a vital part of the company.

Now that you know some great tips on how to mentally prepare yourself for an interview, you can begin anticipating the vital question that would be asked. Your answers to these questions will determine whether you take the next step forward or have to look for opportunities somewhere else.

The next chapters will give you powerful tips to keep in mind when answering the most common interview questions. We will start with the most basic ones and then move on to the more complex behavioral questions that a lot of companies at adopting today to gain greater insight into how you, as an employee, would behave on the job.

CHAPTER 6

Interview Basics

There are some interview questions that have become so common that you can recite the answer off the top of your head. The problem with these questions is that they have been asked by interviewers so many times that they have probably heard all possible versions of the answer. This makes it difficult for you to put a unique spin on your answer that would make it memorable to the one listening to you.

So without further ado, let's dig into those basic interview questions and how to best answer them.

Basic question # 1: Tell me something about yourself

This can be a tricky one. More than trying to get to know you better, you should realize that the interviewer is trying to determine how well you can present numerous ideas concisely and in an engaging manner. When asked such an open ended question, it is so easy to drift away from the main point that you want to drive home and simply ramble on.

The key here is to keep it reasonably short and engaging. Ideally, you should talk about basic information like where you grew up and the degree that you have, and then move on your general work experience and the highlights of your career. You can then move on to some interests or hobbies that you have.

You should note that this is not the time to go into details about projects you've handled and your previous successes. There will be a time to highlight those things. For now, you simply want to let your interviewer know the most basic things about you. Make sure that he or she knows enough that you can move on to something else that you can discuss without having to refer to any notes, canned questions, or your resume.

Basic question # 2: What are your strengths?

Similar to # 1, it would be easy to ramble on when answering this question, especially if you believe that you have a bevy of strengths that you can talk about. Conversely, those who are shy or who lack self-assurance may feel that they have nothing to talk about.

One thing to always remember: Everyone has strengths! You better come to the interview aware of what those strengths are. You can choose two or three attributes that define your work ethic, something along the lines of reliable, hardworking, goal-driven, and tenacious—really, there are countless possibilities.

You can start by stating the particular trait that you consider your strength and they provide an instance in which you exhibit this trait to great advantage. Be confident, but make sure not to border on boasting.

Never be self-deprecating and say you have no strengths. That will surely get you out the door in no time.

Basic question # 3: What are your weaknesses?

Okay, so this is the complete opposite of # 2. It may be tempting to say you think that you have no weaknesses, and that you always see an advantage to everything, or something along those lines, but remember that nobody is perfect, and all of us have probably exhibit some form of shortcoming in the past.

The key here is to be honest. Look back on your past work history, and determine what you could have improved. Maybe you are a supervisor who has difficulty delegating tasks, or maybe you are a worker who has trouble taking criticism. Whatever your weakness is, state it honestly, but always follow up with what steps you have undertaken to ensure that you overcome your weakness.

Basic question # 4: Why did you leave/are you leaving (insert company name here)?

This is another tricky one. Why indeed? You better be downright honest about this one as well. Your choice to leave may have been caused by a conflict, or you may simply be looking for career growth that you can no longer find in your current company. Whatever the reason is, one thing you have to make sure of is never to cast your previous employer in a negative light. Do not use harsh criticism, and never place blame.

If you can be very diplomatic about your answer to this question, chances are that your interviewer would appreciate how you strive to maintain a healthy relationship even with the company and the people that you are leaving behind.

Basic question # 5: Why do you want to work for (insert company name here)?

If you've done your research, then this should not be a problem. Truthfully highlight the great things that you feel the company has to offer, and don't forget to mention how you think you can contribute to making things even better. Just be careful not to overdo it. Sincere appreciation is one thing, but exaggerated flattery is a completely different ballgame.

You can probably state two or three reasons here. Alternatively, if you have one positive thing that you would like to talk about, then you could focus on this particular aspect. Don't forget to relate this advantage with how you think it will help you thrive as an employee of the company if given the opportunity.

So now that we've got the basics out of the way. It's time to discuss the tough cookies—behavioral interview questions.

CHAPTER 7

Answering Behavioral Interview Questions

Behavioral-based interviewing is rapidly gaining ground as the preferred line of questioning during an interview. This approach is based on the theory that the future performance can be most accurately predicted according to previous performance in a similar situation.

Through this interview style, an interviewer can pre-determine whether an applicant possesses the core competencies or skills required to achieve success in a particular job. For this type of questions, the interviewer is not looking for the correct answers because situations always vary. Instead, the interviewer is looking for patterns of behavior that you usually exhibit. Determining such patterns will help in identifying what your likeliest reaction would be and what action you would probably take when confronted with similar situations while on the job.

Be warned, it is very difficult to give a canned answer or fake a previous experience because behavioral interview questions are designed to probe into past scenarios. A seasoned interviewer will surely be able to see whether your story lacks a strong foundation. You can never make up stories on the fly. It is best to answer behavioral interview questions honestly. If you need some time to recall and think about what transpired previously, then you can feel free to ask the interviewer to let you gather your thoughts for a while.

Below you will find 30 of the most common behavioral interview questions and suggested ways by which you can answer them. The questions are divided into five categories to facilitate better understanding.

Leadership

Question # 1: Can you state a time when you accomplished something noteworthy that wouldn't have happened if you had not been there.

When answering this question, avoid using the word "we." While it is true that you have been working with a team at the time, make sure to focus specifically on what you did. Use the word "I" very often. Think about what you felt, what you said, and what you did. Think about a big project to which you made a large contribution, and walk the interviewer through the steps that you took to achieve success.

Question # 2: Can you give me an instance when you were forced to reprimand or fire a friend.

This is difficult because the truth is, you may never have fired or disciplined a friend. What you can do here is to say that you always make it a point to make sure that you and your team are on the same page about the goals you wish to accomplish and that you address any small issue at the first instance that it occurs to prevent the need for disciplining or firing anyone.
Conversely, if you do have experience disciplining or firing a friend, you can talk about why you felt such action was justified and what specific steps you're taken to correct the situation.

Question # 3: Who have you coached or mentored to achieve success?

Now this is a great chance to showcase not only your leadership skills, but your mentoring skills as well. Think of a specific person over whom you have exercised a great deal of influence. Talk about how you inspire this person, how you serve as an example, and how you train him or her to become better at what he or she does. Be sure to relate this to positive results for the company.

Question # 4: Describe for me a time when you may have been disappointed in your behavior.

This question tests how grounded you are and what motivation you have for continuous self-improvement. If you are totally honest with yourself, you could probably think of a time when you felt that you could have done something better. Talk about the experience and how you dealt with it. More importantly, talk about what you will do differently if the same situation arises.

Question # 5: Tell me about a time that you led an important meeting.

This question will also let you touch on your presentation skills. Talk about the time that you had to hold the floor and during a meeting and spearhead a project. Talk about how you prepared, what your agenda was, and what the outcomes were.

Question # 6: Tell me about your leadership style.

This is a broad question and would give you a lot of leeway in providing situations in which you displayed leadership and how your subordinates responded. Think about whether you are a decisive or collaborative leader. You could say that you adopt different styles depending on the situation, but be prepared to provide details on such situations.

Conflict Resolution

Question # 7: Tell me about a time when you were tolerant of an opinion that was different from yours.

Different personalities are bound to have differences in opinion. Recall a time when you felt strongly about something and someone was highly opposed to your idea. Tell the interviewer about how you calmly managed the situation and presented your arguments persuasively.

Question # 8: Tell me about a time that you disagreed with a rule or approach.

This may be difficult to answer because you have to give the impression that you do have a great respect for rules and protocol but you are unafraid to voice out a valid opinion. Talk about the rule and how it was implemented, and be specific about what you disagreed with. Provide details on who you approached and what you said. Whether or not the rule was revised because of your initiative, proving that you are not afraid to question existing processes in a professional manner may give points in your favor.

Question # 9: Tell me something about a team assignment when you had to work with someone difficult.

There's always bound to be someone that you butt your head with at work. However, it does not have to be an aggressive clash of opinions. Talk about how you handled the situation and how you managed to maintain a smooth working relationship. Be careful not to criticize of place any blame here.

Question # 10: Give an example of a time you had to reply to an unhappy boss/client/co-worker.

When you are in customer service, this will probably be an easy one to answer. Talk about what the root of the problem was and what steps you took to ensure that the dissatisfied manager, customer, or colleague felt better about the entire situation.

Question # 11: Was there any instance when you had to resolve a conflict between two colleagues?

This question is designed to determine how well you could act as a mediator or arbiter between two conflicting parties. Talk about how the conflict arose, how you kept a balanced view, how you listened to both sides while reserving judgment, and how you ultimately resolved the conflict and facilitated reconciliation.

Question # 12: Tell me about a time when you disagreed with your boss.

Now this is a question that aims to determine your level of respect for authority. Cite an instance of when you had a difference in opinion with your boss, how you took the initiative to go into further discussion and outline your points, and how you ultimately convinced your boss to look at things your own way.

Initiative and Follow-through

Question # 13: Give me an example of a situation where you had to overcome major obstacles to achieve your objectives.

Your answer should highlight how you persevered and how you never gave up. Not all projects will run smoothly, and talk about what challenges you faced, what actions you took, and how you successfully completed the project despite these issues. You can also highlight your adaptability by saying how you adjusted your plans to be able to overcome obstacles.

Question # 14: Tell me about a time when you won (or lost) an important contract.

You can either highlight the steps you took to succeed or the things that you would have done differently to avoid failure. The important thing here is to put an emphasis on how you take decisive actions and how you deal with their consequences.

Question # 15: What's the most innovative new idea that you have implemented?

Your answer should highlight your creativity and ability to think out of the box. Demonstrate how effectively you can pitch new ideas and how courageous you are in trying to break from the mold and propose something completely new.

Question # 16: Tell me about a time when you came up with a new approach to a problem.

Answer in such a way that you show your willingness to divert from the tried and true approached and your openness to try new things to deal with a problem. Talk about your thought process as you came up with a new approach, and share how you implemented this idea for the benefit of your team.

Question # 17: Tell me about a goal that you set that took a long time to achieve or that you are still working towards.

Your answer should highlight your tenacity—your ability to set a goal, formulate a plan, and stick to it despite any delays. Timetables are mere guides and are not set in stone. Talk about how you adopted and how you saw the project through to the end.

Question # 18: Tell me about a time that you identified a need and went above and beyond the call of duty to get things done.

Your answer should highlight your willingness to go the extra mile just to ensure that your project becomes a success. Talk about the goals, and then talk about what you did to exceed those goals.

Teamwork

Question # 19: Give me an example of a team project that failed.

Give the interviewer insight into how you play into the dynamics of your team. Highlight how well you collaborate with others, how you can stick to a plan, and how you strive to do your part. Also detail how you deal with failure and how you keep the team motivated despite a setback.

Question # 20: Can you tell me about a time when you were able to understand another person and guide your actions by your understanding of their individual needs or values?

Highlight how you have shown your regard for others and how you recognize that a team is only as strong as its weakest member. Detail how you were able to show professional concern and how you provided support to a colleague.

Question # 21: What did you do in your last job to contribute toward a teamwork environment?

Be specific in answering this question, and keep the word "recent" in mind. This would show that you exhibit collaborative behavior consistently under any circumstance.

Question # 22: Describe how you developed rapport with your peers and your supervisor.

This is an important question in that it enables you to show that you can build relationships at all organizational levels. Make sure that you provide situational examples of both cases, and highlight what you think about the importance of goal alignment and cooperation.

Question # 23: Tell me about a time when you were on a team and one of your teammates was not doing his or her part.

Highlight your diplomacy and consideration here. Talk about how you determined the problem, spoke to your teammate, and took the necessary actions to ensure that everyone equally contributed to the team. Talk about how you resolved the problem with your colleague without needing the intervention of your boss or human resources.

Question # 24: Share a rewarding team experience.

You can probably speak at length about this topic. You can talk about one of your greatest team successes, what your role was, and how you coordinated with everyone involved to achieve significant results.

Problem Solving and Decision Making

Question # 25: Describe for me a time when you had to make an important decision with limited facts.

Highlight your power of inference. Talk about how you analyzed trends and considered statistics to determine the best course of action. Talk about the input you required, and detail whether the decision ended up being the right one.

Question # 26: Tell me about a time when you were forced to make an unpopular decision.

Your answer should highlight all the pros and cons that you had to consider when making the decision. Talk about why many were opposed to the decision, and why you think it was still justified to take the action that you did.

Question # 27: Describe a time when you anticipated potential problems and developed preventive measures.

This question will enable you to talk about your foresight. Detail what the problem was, as well as what preventive measures you took. Specify why you chose those measures and how effective they were in preventing the problem from occurring.

Question # 28: If you had to do that activity over again, how would you do it differently?

This is your opportunity to discuss something that you did which you think you could have improved on. Talk about the level of success you achieved and why you feel you could have done better. Share details on what differences you will implement to ensure improved outcomes.

Question # 29: Tell me about a time when you made a bad decision.

This may be a bit difficult to talk about, but be as honest as you can. Talk about what the project was, what went wrong, why you failed to foresee the failure, and how you felt at the aftermath. You could then segue into what you did to prevent failure going forward.

Question # 30: Provide an example of a time in which you had to use your fact-finding skills to gain information for solving a problem.

Use your answer to highlight your ability to conduct research, filter information, and identify the data that you need to make a good decision. Talk about the resources that you used, the people you spoke with, and the things you considered. You can then move on to discuss how all your efforts paid off and help you make the right decision.

Now that you have the most powerful tips to ace your interview, your arsenal is fully stocked as you endeavor to land that dream job. Remember that answering questions with candor and having confidence in your abilities will go a long way in making sure that you double your chances for success.

Conclusion

Thank you again for purchasing this book! I really do hope you found it helpful.

If you did, then I'd like to ask you for a favor, would you be kind enough to leave a review for this book on Amazon? It'd be greatly appreciated!

Thank you and good luck!

www.ingramcontent.com/pod-product-compliance
Lightning Source LLC
Chambersburg PA
CBHW020956180526
45163CB00006B/2396